Established in 2011, Shia Rights Watch (SRW) is the world's first independent organization dedicated to define and protect the rights of Shia Muslims around the world. SRW is a non- governmental, not-for-profit research entity and advocacy group headquartered in Washington D.C., U.S.A. Shia Rights Watch holds a 501(c) status, as well as holding a Special consultation status (ECOSOC) with the United Nations. Shia Rights Watch aims to draw the international attention where Shia rights are violated; the aim is to give a voice to the oppressed and hold oppressors accountable for their crimes.

S.R.W. achieves its objectives through strategic investigations supported by targeted advocacy in order to bring about informed action.

.

Vision

Freedom of religion for all

Shia Rights Watch envisions the world with peace for all humans, regardless of their religion, gender, race and origin. There should be regulations in every country to support every religion. We believe Shia Muslim as religion should be recognized in every country and any discrimination should be brought to light. God has given us all the freedom of religion and the rights to live in peace.

Mission

No Shia above the law and no Shia Below the law

Shia Rights Watch is dedicated to protect the rights of Shia Muslims worldwide. We investigate violations against Shia communities in order to raise awareness against injustice. We promote the change through research and publications. Our reports and articles are submitted to the governments and international organizations, and we continually monitor media outlets to ensure coverage of Shia rights violations. Shia Rights Watch stands for victims of prejudice, and supports activism in order to prevent discrimination, support political freedom, and protect people from inhumane conduct. We enlist the local public and international communities to support the cause of human rights for all.

The Purpose of SRW

Shia Muslims face constant oppression throughout the world solely based on their faith. In some countries, Shia Muslims have been the target of repeated persecution for centuries as evidenced in the well-documented expansion of extremism of the Wahhabi movement. We believe the underrepresented Shia Muslim population need a human rights organization that highlights the violations against them, while giving their call for help a louder voice.

Staff Organization

The organization began with the collaborative efforts of volunteers with a common interest in advocating international human rights. The momentum created by the increasing number of volunteer and activism allowed for a formal development of the foundation of Shia Rights Watch. Currently the organization has more than 100 active members working in various locations worldwide. The responsibilities of members range from gathering news and information to publishing reports and articles in order to advocate change. We are proud of the religiously and ethnically diverse group of activists who are working together towards a common goal.

Methodology of SRW

We believe that information is the most valuable resource in the investigative process. From the organization's inception, we have focused on gathering information through various media: interviewing witnesses, family members of the victims and victims themselves; on-site collection of resources; analyzing reports from various national and international organizations; meeting with non-governmental and religious organizations, leaders, and journalists; and creating information networks in a wide range of social sectors.

Based on the information collected from the above sources, different types of human rights violation have been identified. These violations include but are certainly not limited to:

Violation of right of living;

Arbitrary arrest, unfair trial, and illegal detention;

Psychical & psychological abuse: torture, rape, and sexual assault;

Illegal confiscation of private property;

Demolition of Religions centers;

Employment discrimination;

Education discrimination;

Reports, Publications, and Distribution

Whether it is terrorist bombings of sacred shrines, torture and unjust detention of people, discriminative legislation or intimation of school children for their sectarian beliefs, Shia have been victimized in most the world. In countries where the press is tightly controlled, most of these cases go unnoticed. Shia Rights Watch tells the stories of injustices and atrocities in order to give a voice to the marginalized Shia victims.

Journalists investigating topics regarding the Middle East will benefit from SRW's focus on the Shia communities since they are crucially important sectors in Middle Eastern society. For instance, In order to fully examine the ongoing atrocities committed against protesters of the Arab spring, it is necessary to know about the embedded Shia struggle. In areas where Shia have been formerly discriminated against more subtly, the Arab Spring opened a door for more blunt persecution. Cases reported in other parts of the world, such as in South Asia, describe violence and intimidation which reflect fluctuating trends in sectarian hostilities, fueled by various political issues, including terrorism. SRW's aim is to be able to report the crimes affecting Shia in every part of the globe.

SRW has investigators on the forefront who communicate directly with the victims and monitor multilingual news media outlets. SRW networks with national committees, international human rights organizations, as well as religious scholars of Shia communities. SRW's members comprise of people with diverse ethnic and religious backgrounds united to defend the human rights. This international network provides invaluable information to commentators and journalists of the media who are seeking to explore the impact of events on the Shia communities worldwide.

 shiarightswatch   shiarightswatch   shiarightswatch   shiarightswatch

Shia Rights Watch envisions the world with peace for all humans, regardless of their religion, gender, race and origin. There should be regulations in every country to support every religion. We believe Shia Muslim as religion should be recognized in every country and any discrimination should be brought to light. God has given us all the freedom of religion and the rights to live in peace.

Shia Rights Watch

1050 17th St NW Suite 800

Washington, DC 20036

Tel: +1 (202) 350 4302 Or 202-643 SHIA

srwdc@ShiaRightsWatch.org

CONTENTS

SUMMARY

Pakistan is suffering a major crisis, in which terrorist groups are committing mass events of violence. The living conditions of the minorities get worse in recent years, at least 210 members of the Shia Muslim population were killed in targeted attacks that took place across Pakistan; around half of the killings took place at neighboring provinces of Balochistan and Sindh. Most of these attacks are carried by the local terrorist organizations of Lashkar-e-Jhangvi (LeJ) and Sipah-e-Sahaba (SeS). Most of the attacks are carried on sectarian grounds, as LeJ and SeS consider Shia Muslims as infidels. According to the groups who consider Shias as infidels, Shia Muslims have been given too much importance, and being given senior positions- scholars, doctors, lawyers, politicians. Terrorist organizations mostly target Shia scholars, activists or those who have senior positions.

This report aims to highlight some of the attacks and killings and emphasize on urgent need of change in the Pakistan.

Shia Rights Watch (SRW) believes The government of Pakistan should follow up on his public denunciations of sectarian killings by ordering the immediate arrest and prosecution of the leadership of the LeJ, its members, and affiliates responsible for planning sectarian violence. The government should immediately remove from service any administrative or security personnel implicated in sectarian attacks or who failed to investigate and arrest alleged perpetrators of such attacks and take extra security measures in Balochistan and Sindh provinces as the majority of the terrorist attacks against Shias take place in these provinces.

The international actors, such as the US, EU, UN, IMF, etc. should press the Pakistani government to uphold its international human rights obligations and promote good governance by investigating sectarian killings in Shia dominant areas and prosecuting all those responsible, particularly the LeJ leadership. They should offer to support external law enforcement assistance with investigations into sectarian killings in Shia dominant areas.

The non-governmental organizations should be responsible of restoring and preserving the destroyed Shia mosques and shrines. They should initiate human rights training, religious tolerance and promote dialogue between the Sunnis and Shias.

BACKGROUND

The Islamic Republic of Pakistan is a sovereign country in Southeast Asia bordered by the Arabian Sea and the Gulf of Oman to the south, Iran to the southwest, Afghanistan to the west and north, India to the east, and China to the far northeast.

With a population of over 188 million, Pakistan is the sixth most populated country in the world, following China, India, the United States, Indonesia, and Brazil. The country's largest cities are Karachi, Lahore, Faisalabad, and Rawalpindi, with the city of Islamabad as the capital.

In 1985, Pakistan's constitution adopted a federal parliamentary system, calling for a president as head of state and an elected prime minister as head of the government. Currently, the president of the republic is Mamnoon Hussain and the prime minister is Nawaz Hussain, both elected in 2013.

RELIGION IN PAKISTAN

Pakistan is religiously divided by Muslims making up 96.3% of the population and Christians, Hindus, and others making up the remaining 3.7%. Of the 96.3 percent, the Shia community makes up roughly 20%, with the Sunni community consisting of over 75 percent of the country's ever-growing population[1]

In the separation from India and formation of the new country, Pakistan struggled under the Two-Nation theory that Muslims and Hindus cannot exist together. Although for centuries they have lived together, they could never forget that they had their own culture and way of civilization that could never mesh with the other religion. Muslims came to realize all of their differences from the Hindu community and argued that their electoral grounds should be separate, and so they were. But it simply didn't end on a Muslim-Hindu break, because inside the Muslim community, Shia and Sunni were separated with given rights.

WHO ARE THE SHIA MUSLIMS?

Shia Muslims are followers of the rightful successors of Prophet Mohammad, appointed by Prophet Mohammad himself as his successors. They believe in the basic instructors of Islamic teachings and rulers in the name of Islam.

Shia Muslims today present as much as half the population of Muslims all around the world and their history has been brilliant since the dawn of Islam. Shia's knowledge is well spread in the world through countless writings and publications as well as through the foundation of a great number of religious and scientific schools, colleges, institutions and libraries- all led by top professional and religious scholars and preachers.

These foundations are located worldwide and basically in a number of holy cities like Najaf, Karbala, Kathimiya, Samarra, Qom, Mashad; capitals like Beirut, Cairo, Baghdad, Karachi, Jakarta, Kuwait, Qatar, Damascus and Tehran; cities like al Ihsa' and al Khatif in Saudi Arabia; countries like Afghanistan, Libya, Tunisia, Algeria, Jordon, and many others.

Shia Muslims believe in 5 pillars of Islam that are monotheistic, Prophet-hood, and leadership of the twelve Imams appointed by Prophet Mohammad, Justice, and Day of Judgment.

Shia as monotheist believes in:

• Allah as being the One and the All-Just,

[1] "Field Listing: Religions, Pakistan," *Central Intelligence Agency*, Retrieved on January 8, 2015, https://www.cia.gov/library/publications/the-world-factbook/fields/2122.html?countryName=Pakistan&countryCode=pk&regionCode=sas&#pk.

- Mohammad as Allah's Messenger and Prophet and who has appointed the twelve Imams as successors (starting from Imam Ali up till Imam Mahdi),

- Islam as a religion,

- Quran as the Holy Book, in Kab'ba as a Qibla (the direction that should be faced during prayer),

- Existence of Heaven and Hell,

- Prophet Mohammad's entire divine teachings.

Shia follows the Islamic standards of allowed or permitted deeds and avoid prohibited ones.

Shia Muslims believe:

- In Islam as a complete religion through which human beings may reach all potentials and happiness in both world; here and in the hereafter.

- In unity of all Muslims. Think that internal differences that have led to divisions between Muslim sects should be solved according to the Quran and the Divine teachings of Prophet Mohammad peace be upon him and his household, void of any intolerance and violence.

- In brotherhood ties between human beings, regardless of race, culture, citizenship and color.

- In equality in citizenship as well as duties and rights between man and woman.

According to Shia Muslims, the foundation and establishment of an Islamic rule, regime or state is only achieved with the presence and the leadership of the twelfth Imam, Mohammad al Mahdi, who brings justice to all human beings especially oppressed people in this world.

- Shia Muslims pay their maximum efforts to achieve freedom, dignity, justice and equality.

- Shia strongly believes that violence and terrorism have nothing to do with the religion and they try their best to achieve their civilized goals through peace and nonviolence.

- Politically, Shia Muslims believe in plurality, democracy and openness to all, that is why acceptance is highly granted in Shiism.

Finally, Shia Muslims believe that thought and religion overcomes any geographical boundaries. Shiism is a multicultural faith and Shia Muslims are independent from any geographical and political region.

SHIA POPULATION OF PAKISTAN

With a population of over 188 million in Pakistan, Shia Muslims make up over 36 million. Although the Shia make up the minority in Pakistan, they make their presence known as leaders in political positions as well as in the important roles that they play in their country's independence, history, and the building of their nation. The single most important Shia figure in the history of Pakistan is Muhammad Ali Jinah, the Qaid Azam ("the Great Founder"), the founder of the state of Pakistan. In Pakistan Shias have been elected to top offices and played an important part in the country's social and political arena.

Besides Muhammed Ali Jinah, some of the most renowned Shias of Pakistan is as such:

- Muhammad Ali Bogra- Prime Minister, Minister of Foreign Affairs, and Minister of Defense[2].

---

[2] "Muhammed Ali Bogra," *Bogra.org*. Retrieved on January 3, 2015, *http://www.bogra.org/bogra1.html*.

- Khawaja Nazimuddin- Prime Minister, Governor General, and Minister of Defense[3].

The Bhutto family- Pakistani political family which has been dominant in the Pakistan People's Party (PPP). Some notable members are Shah Nawaz Bhutto, Zulfikar Ali Bhutto, Nusrat Bhutto, Benazir Bhutto, Fatima Bhutto including Benazir Bhutto's husband, Asif Ali Zardari, 11th President and co-chair of PPP[4].

- Syeda Abida Hussain- Pakistan Ambassador to the United States, Member of the National Assembly[5].
- Mushahid Hussain Syed- Secretary General of Pakistan Muslim League, Ministry of Information and Media Broadcasting, Ministry of Telecommunications[6].
- Faisal Saleh Hayat- Minister of Interior[7].
- Farzana Raja- Member of the National Assembly[8].
- Fahmida Mirza- Speaker of the National Assembly and her husband Zulfiqar Mirza- Politician of PPP[9].
- Mushaf Ali Mir- Chief of Air Staff[10].
- Tanveer Naqvi- Three-star general of Pakistan Army[11].
- Yahya Khan- 3rd President, Minister of Foreign Affairs, Minister of Defense, Chief of Army Staff[12].
- Muhammad Musa- 10th Governor of Balochistan, 4th Governor of West Pakistan, 4th Army Commander-in-Chief[13].
- Iskander Mirza- 1st President, Governor-General, Minister of the Interior, Governor of East Bengal, 1st Defense Secretary[14].

TERRORISM IN TODAY'S PAKISTAN

The most well-known terrorist groups in Pakistan today are Lashkar-e-Jhangvi (LeJ) and Sipah-e-Sahaba(SeS), also known as Ahle Sunnat Wal Jamaat(ASWJ) when banded together.

The LeJ formed in 1996 as a breakaway terrorist group from SeS, blaming the parent group of going into an opposite direction than Maulana Haq Nawaz Jhangvi, their co-founder, had planned for the militant group[15]. It is from the SeS co-founder that they named their branch group, but it is LeJ's cofounder, Malik Ishaq, that has made his presence known throughout the years. In 1997, Ishaq was arrested on charges for murder, death threats, and intimidation. In 2009, authorities said that the attack by LeJ on the Sri Lankan cricket team that killed eight and injured seven plus the assistant coach in Lahore, was set into motion by Ishaq himself from his prison cell[16]. During his time in prison, he admitted to many crimes, but was released due to lack of evidence in July 2011. This year, the United States placed Ishaq on the Global Terrorist list on February 7th[17].The Pakistani government declared LeJ to be a terrorist group in 2001, and was banned by 2011, although they still operate very openly.

LeJ's parent group, SeS, was formed in September of 1985 in a community that already had a rise in sectarian violence. The SeS has been aiming to protect the Sunnis and their law while getting Pakistan to declare themselves a Sunni state. They have marked down Shias as non-Muslim and complaining that they have been given too much importance, always showing up on the television, the radio, newspapers, and being given senior positions (scholars, doctors, lawyers, politicians). They are known to

[3] "Khawajaa Nazimuddin," *Story of Pakistan*. Retrieved January 3, 2015, http://storyofpakistan.com/khawaja-nazimuddin/.
[4] "Zulfikar Ali Bhutto," *Pakistan Herald*. Retrieved January 8, 2015, http://www.pakistanherald.com/profile/zulfikar-ali-bhutto-1182.
[5] John Wilson, "Pakistan: The Struggle Within," *Peason Longman, 2009*, 5.
[6] "Takfiri terrorist planned to hit 21 Pakistani Shia scholars, politicians, and Iranian envoy," *Shia Post*. October 29, 2014, http://en.shiapost.com/2014/10/29/takfiri-terrorist-planned-to-hit-21-pakistan-shia-scholars-politicians-and-iranian-envoy/.
[7] "Makhdoom Syed Faisal Saleh Hayat," *Awaz TV*, Retrieved January 8, 2015, http://www.awaztoday.com/singleprofile/82/Makhdoom-Syed-Faisal-Saleh-Hayat.aspx.
[8] "Farzana Raja Politician of PPP," *Blog Post. Retrieved January 8, 2015, http://www.chatdd.com/blog/fashion-lifestyle/farzana-raja-politician-of-pakistan-peoples-party/.
[9] "The untold story of Shia Muslims in Pakistan," *Blog Post*, Retrieved on January 8, 2015, http://theterrorland.blogspot.com/2011/12/untold-story-of-shia-muslims-in.html.
[10] "PAF s' Chief of the Air Staffs, Air Chief Marshal Mushaf Ali Mir (Shaheed)," *Paffalcons*, Retrieved on January 8, 2015, http://www.paffalcons.com/cas/mushaf-ali-mir.php.
[11] "Shiism and sectarian conflict in Pakistan," *Blog Post*, Retrieved on January 8, 2015, https://chainsoff.wordpress.com/2014/09/12/shiasim-and-sectarian-conflict-in-pakistan/.
[12] Va'i Nasr, "The Shia Revival: How Conflicts Within Islam Will Shape the Future," *W. W. Norton, 2006*, 88-90.
[13] "Shiism and sectarian conflict in Pakistan".
[14] "Shiism and sectarian conflict in Pakistan".
[15] "Lashkar-e-Jhangvi," *South Asia Terrorism Portal*. Retrieved from http://www.satp.org/satporgtp/countries/pakistan/terroristoutfits/lej.htm.
[16] "2009 Cricket Team Attack," *Telegraph*. http://www.telegraph.co.uk/news/worldnews/asia/pakistan/9511292/Mastermind-behind-Sri-Lanka-cricket-team-attack-arrested.html.
[17] "Ishaq Named Global Terrorist," *Dawn*. http://www.dawn.com/news/1085321.

mainly operate in two ways, targeting prominent activists of opposing organizations and firing on the Shia worshippers inside mosques[18].

In an overview of the year 2013, the Human Rights Coalition of Pakistan reported over 200 Shia deaths in Balochistan in the first few weeks of the year as an end result to sectarian violence, over 200 attacks for the entire year that killed almost 700 and left hundreds upon hundreds injured.19 Over 90% of these attacks occurred in Quetta, Karachi, Kangu, Parachinar, Islamabad, and Rawalpindi[20].

On December 9, the Coalition for the Rights of Minorities Pakistan (CRMP) has urged the government to check the growing intolerance in country on emergency basis. In a press release, the CRMP Coordinator Sameena Imtiaz said human rights violations had seen a surge during the tenure of the present government while religious freedom had been curtailed. She said the federal and the provincial governments had failed to put in place effective mechanisms in place for the protection and promotion of minorities. The national coordinator for CRMP pointed to the widespread targeted violence against religious and ethnic minorities including targeted killings of Sikh community members in KP, Shia Hazaras in Quetta, Hindu community in Sindh and Christians in Punjab[21].

Similarly, Minority Rights Group International, a UK-based nongovernmental organization, expresses concern about Pakistan's treatment of its minorities. The organization's latest report, Searching for Security: the Rising Marginalization of Religious Communities in Pakistan, released on Dec. 9, says Ahmadis, Christian and Hindus "live in daily fear of harassment and intimidation" and that "escalating violence against Shia Muslims also points to the growth of an even more exclusionary form of nationalism based on a very specific understanding of 'Muslim-ness'. [22]

Deputy Secretary General of Majlis-e-Wahdat-e-Muslimeen, Allama Amin Shaheedi, stated that 160 Shia Muslims were killed during 2014 (January to September) and among them were 3 eminent scholars, 5 doctors, 5 engineers, 3 professors, 5 lawyers, 21 traders, 90 students and youths, and police officials. Allama Shaheedi said that Shia notables and traders were targeted because the terrorists saw government's inaction as a green signal to them to continue Shia genocide[23]. According to a report released by the independent Human Rights Commission of Pakistan, over 300,000 Pakistani people have fled the unrest in the country's southwestern Balochistan Province since 2004[24]. Pakistani media is usually quiet over the killings of Shia. The newspapers briefly flash the killings on their web sites, and most of the time these incidents do not take place in the paper formats of the newspapers.

In order to protect the lives of the Shia Muslims, Shia Rights Watch sent a letter to President Barack Obama requesting his assistance in protecting the rights of Shia throughout the Middle East and South Asia. In this letter, the organization calls for Pakistan to be added to the U.S. Department of State's list of countries of particular concern because of the lack of protection for Shia communities. Shia Rights Watch also calls for the Administration to voice its support for Congressional action stating support for Shia Muslims throughout this region. Shia Rights specifically names Ahl-e-Sunnat-Wal-Jammat (ASWJ), and ISIS as the two groups responsible for the murder of hundreds of Shia this year alone.

With such a strong presence of these extremist groups, Shia Muslims are never safe in Pakistan. A quick trip down to the grocery store, an afternoon worshipping session at the mosque, or a pilgrimage into Iran can turn into never returning home again. Innocent Shias are attacked on the streets because others do not agree with their religion, and the government is doing little to nothing to protect them and their rights.

18 "Sipah-e-Sahaba," South Asia Terrorism Portal. Retrieved from http://www.satp.org/satporgtp/countries/pakistan/terroristoutfits/ssp.htm.
19 "Human Rights Coalition of Pakistan 2013 Overview," Retrieved from http://www.hrcp-web.org/hrcpweb/report14/AR2013.pdf.
20 "Who's Killing Pakistan's Shia and Why?" Retrieved from http://warontherocks.com/2014/05/whos-killing-pakistans-shia-and-why/.
21 "CRMP urges govt to check growing intolerance," International News Network. December 9, 2014, http://www.onlinenews.com.pk/details.php?newsid=278693&catname=Pakistan.
22 "A new report confirms the bad news about pakistan's non-Sunni citizens," NewsWeek Pakistan. December 9, 2014, http://newsweekpakistan.com/protecting-its-minorities-pakistans-real-test/.
23 "Pakistan: Shia genocide not sectarian issue but ferocious takfiri terrorists, 160 Shia killed in one year," ABNA. September 9, 2014, http://www.abna.ir/english/service/centeral-asia-subcontinent/archive/2014/09/09/636487/story.html.
24 "300,000 Pakistanis fled Balochistan since 2004, " Press TV. October 15, 2014. http://www.presstv.ir/detail/2014/10/15/382351/300000-pakistanis-fled-balochistan/.

As a member of the United Nations, Pakistan agreed to the Universal Declaration of Human Rights (UDHR) that was passed in 1948, meaning that they were to be held responsible for providing everyone equal human rights. Even though they agreed to the UDHR and were to uphold those rules, SRW has found many human rights violations toward the Shia in Pakistan. This report aims to highlight these inhuman violations of 2014.

January 1: Passenger bus carrying fifty Shia Muslims returning from a pilgrimage to Iran is targeted by a suicide car bombing killing two Shia and wounding seventeen, including four policemen[25].

January 6: 14-year-old student, Itizaz Hassan, was martyred when he confronted a suicide bomber planning to attack his school. The incident occurred in the Shia-dominated area in the Hangu district[26]. Hassan later went on to be recognized as a hero and nominated for awards, as well as having the school and its stadium named after him.

January 15: 35-year-old Chartered Accountant, Ali Hussain Qazilbash, shot two times in the chest and killed by unidentified motorcyclists at a traffic light in Lahore[27].

January 16: The Tablighi Markaz center in Peshawar was bombed during evening prayers, killing eight and injuring 67 others. The bomb was found in a canister of cooking oil, while two other bombs were diffused on site[28].

January 20: Allama Alim al-Musvi, prominent Shia leader, was attacked and killed by two gunmen who fired at him in the alley as he was leaving his home to go to the mosque. The attackers fled before police could seal off the area[29].

January 21: At least 22 killed and more than two dozen injured when a bus convoy returning from Iran pilgrimage was attacked by bombing[30].

January 26: Bomb detonation near a playground in Hangu leaves six children dead and many others injured[31].

January 30: KDA College vice Principal Syed Asghar Hussain Zaidi killed and wife injured by ASWJ on their way home from their weekly religious gathering[32].

February 4: At least 9, mostly Shia, were killed and 25 others wounded in a Peshawar hotel, mostly frequented by Shia, in a suspected suicide attack; Taliban later claimed responsibility[33].

February 16: Well-known Shia scholar, Tayyaba Khanam Bukhari, leaves Pakistan after threats were made on her life continuously by an unknown group. Last year, she had been attacked, but luckily received no wounds. After contacting authorities for help and getting nothing in return, the scholar decided to leave the country in order to protect her life[34].

March 3: Just a few days after the TTP announced a ceasefire, eleven were killed and many more injured in an attack on an Islamabad court. Two of the attackers were suicide bombers, and the others threw hand grenades and open-fired on the courtroom, though it is believed that they were targeting certain people seeing as that a female lawyer and the judge were killed[35].

March 14: Taliban group carries out two attacks. Ten killed and more than thirty injured in Quetta when a bomb, targeting a Frontier Corps vehicle, went off near a passenger bus. The second attack occurred in Peshawar when a suicide bomber blast went off near an armored police vehicle, killing nine and wounding thirty[36].

[25] "Pakistan car bombing kills Shia pilgrims," *Al Jazeera News*. January 1, 2014, http://www.aljazeera.com/news/asia/2014/01/pakistan-car-bombing-kills-shia-pilgrims-201411164239145555.html.
[26] "Shia student embraced martyrdom foiling suicidal attack on school in Hangu," *Shia Post*. January 6, 2014, http://en.shiapost.com/2014/01/06/shia-student-embraced-martyrdom-foiling-suicidal-attack-on-school-in-hangu/.
[27] "Shia Muslim Ali Hussain Qazilbash shot martyred in Lahore," *Shia Post*. January 16, 2014, http://en.shiapost.com/2014/01/16/shia-muslim-ali-hussain-qazilbash-shot-martyred-in-lahore/.
[28] "Blast at Peshawar Tablighi centre kills ten, injures more than 60," *Dawn*. January 16, 2014, http://www.dawn.com/news/1080731/.
[29] "Gunmen shoot and kill Shia leader in Peshawar," *Press TV*. January 20, 2014, http://www.presstv.com/detail/2014/01/20/346756/gunmen-shoot-dead-shia-leader-in-peshawar/.
[30] "Bomb targets bus of Shia pilgrims in south-west Pakistan," *BBC News*. January 21, 2014, http://www.bbc.com/news/world-asia-25832979.
[31] "Bomb explosion kills six Shia children in Pakistani town of Hangu," *Press TV*. January 26, 2014, http://www.presstv.com/detail/2014/01/26/347860/blast-kills-6-shia-children-in-pakistan/.
[32] "ASWJ terrorists kill Shia educationist, injure his wife in Karachi," *Shia Post*. January 31, 2014, http://en.shiapost.com/2014/01/31/aswj-terrorists-kill-shia-educationist-injure-his-wife-in-karachi/.
[33] "Nine killed in blast in Pakistan's Shia-dominated area of Peshawar," *NDTV*. February 4, 2014, http://www.ndtv.com/article/world/nine-killed-in-blast-in-pakistan-s-shia-dominated-area-of-peshawar-479307.
[34] "Pakistan famous lady Shia scholar leaves country after multiple life threats," *Shafaqna*. February 17, 2014, http://en.shafaqna.com/topnews/item/25621-pakistan-famous-lady-shia-scholar-leaves-country-after-multiple-life-threats.html.
[35] "Islamabad court suicide attack strikes terrorism blow in Pakistani capital," *The Guardian*. March 3, 2014, http://www.theguardian.com/world/2014/mar/03/islamabad-court-suicide-attack-terrorism-pakistani-capital.
[36] "Nearly two dozen people killed in attacks across Pakistan," *Shia Post*. March 14, 2014, http://en.shiapost.com/2014/03/14/nearly-two-dozen-people-killed-in-attacks-across-pakistan/.

April 8: At least seventeen dead and 46 others wounded when a bomb went off on a passenger train on its way to Rawalpindi. Five children were believed to be amongst the dead. A separatist group called the United Baluch Army claimed responsibility on the attack[37].

April 9: 50-year-old Syed Haider Raza shot three times and killed by unidentified gunmen as he was getting into his car when leaving work. He was in charge of the ER and was a university professor[38].

April 10: Taxi driver, Mohammad Karam, was stopped by Taliban militants, pulled out of the vehicle upon finding out he was Shia, and shot him sporadically[39].

April 12: Two Shia were singled out on a passenger bus by armed militants and shot, killing one instantly, and the other succumbing to wounds when being transferred to a hospital[40].

April 25: Blast outside a Shia mosque, targeting Shia notables and students on a passenger bus, killed four and injured more than thirty others in Karachi. The 10kg bomb was planted in a rickshaw mixed with ball bearings and nut bolts[41].

May 11: Five killed and 14 others injured when a suicide bomber entered the Arbab Niaz stadium and fired gunshots. Security personnel retaliated and fired back, when the suicide bomber detonated his explosives near a mosque in the stadium. The blast knocked down one of the mosque's walls and damaged nearby buildings[42].

May 15: Shia youth, Mubarak Ali Shan, was returning home when confronted by five LeJ/ASWJ militants. They shot at him, but the youth fell to the ground in enough time, causing the bullet to hit one of their own men, leaving Shan unharmed[43].

May 31: Imambargah Moosa Kazim's custodian, Ali Raza, was slaughtered by the ASWJ with an axe[44].

June 8: At least 24 were killed and 14 others injured in an attack carried out by four suicide bombers on two adjacent hotels on the Pakistan-Iran border where Shia pilgrims were staying the night[45].

June 18: ASWJ trespassed and killed a family of eight Internally Displaced Persons (IDPs) in Hangu[46].

August 12: Two Shia men, including a doctor, were gunned down in separate attacks in Karachi[47].

August 13: A senior police officer, Ghazanfer Kazmi, was shot to dead in Karachi.

56-year-old Dr. Amir Mehdi was also shot to dead by two assailants riding on a motorcycle that fired shots and rode away.

40-year-old Abbas Haider Zaidi was also shot to dead by assailants riding motorcycles.

August 16: Kazim Raza, 45, and his 22-year-old daughter Neha Fatima died on the spot when four unidentified attackers opened fire at the family outside their house near the Dar-e-Batool Imambargah in Surjani Town.

August 19: Two Shia men, 34-year-old Syed Kashif Hussain Rizvi and 55-year-old Khwaja Bajshish Hussain Ansari were gunned down by motorcyclists affiliated to SeS near Qalandria Chowk.

In Hussainabad, were injured when unidentified motorcyclists opened fire at a bakery within the jurisdiction of the Azizabad police station. The injured were taken to Abbasi Shaheed Hospital where the Shia man Fida Hussain, 35, and his Sunni friend Zeeshan Ali, 30, succumbed to their injuries during treatment. 2 other Shias namely Akhtar Hussain and Mumtaz are still in the hospital.

[37] "Train bombing in Pakistan's Baluchistan province kills at least 17," *LA Times*. April 8, 2014, ttp://www.latimes.com/world/worldnow/la-fg-wn-pakistan-train-bombing-20140408-story.html.
[38] "Shia doctor gunned down in Karachi," *Pakistan Today*. April 9, 2014, http://www.pakistantoday.com.pk/2014/04/09/national/shia-doctor-gunned-down-in-karachi/.
[39] "Shia taxi driver was martyred by Yazidi takfiri terrorists near Parachinar," *Shia Markaz*. April 10, 2014, http://shiamarkaz.com/shia-taxi-driver-was-martyred-by-yazidi-takfiri-terrorists-near-parachinar/.
[40] "Two Shia Hazaras gunned down in Quetta," *Dawn News*. April 12, 2014, http://www.dawn.com/news/1099414.
[41] "Shia Muslims were target of the terrorists who killed 4 in Karachi blast," *Shiite News*. April 25, 2014, http://www.shiitenews.com/index.php/pakistan/9781-shia-muslims-were-target-of-the-terrorists-who-killed-4-karachi-ites-in-blast.
[42] "Five killed, 14 injured in Pakistan suicide blast," *Zee News*. May 11, 2014, http://zeenews.india.com/news/south-asia/five-killed-14-injured-in-pakistan-suicide-blast_931432.html.
[43] "Shia youth escapes unhurt in Yazidi terrorist attack in Quetta," *Shiite News*. May 15, 2014, http://www.shiitenews.com/index.php/pakistan/10030-shia-youth-escapes-unhurt-in-yazidi-terrorist-attack-in-quetta.
[44] "Custodian of Imambargh slaughtered in Karachi," *Shia Post*. May 31, 2014, http://en.shiapost.com/2014/05/31/custodian-of-imambargh-slaughtered-in-karachi/.
[45] "Jaish-ul-Islam claims attack on Shia pilgrims," *Newsweek*. June 8, 2014, http://newsweekpakistan.com/jaish-ul-islam-claims-attack-on-shia-pilgrims/.
[46] "ASWJ Terrorists kill 8 Shia IDPS of a family in Hangu," *Shia Post*. June 18, 2014, http://en.shiapost.com/2014/06/18/aswj-terrorists-kill-8-shia-idps-of-a-family-in-hangu/.
[47] "A Doctor, a senior police officer among three Shiite shot dead in Pakistan," *AhlulBayt News Agency (ABNA)*. August 12, 2014, http://www.abna.ir/english/service/central-asia-subcontinent/archive/2014/08/13/630812/story.html.

August 29: A Shia is shot to dead by SeS terrorists in Karachi.

A Shia, Ghulam Baqar, is critically wounded in Liaquatabad[48].

August 30: Dr Aun Naseem Jafri, a Shia physician of Korangi's Zaman Town, was the latest victim of a gun attack on Thursday. He martyred two weeks after the murder of a colleague in the same fashion in his clinic in Landhi[49].

September 7: Syed Yasir Ali Tirmizi and Kashif Hussain were shot to dead by terrorists of Lashkar-e-Jhangvi in Karachi[50].

September 8: Gunmen have killed three people, including a senior military official, Brigadier Fazal Zahoor, his brother Fazal Subhani. The third person is identified as Mohammad Ayub. The incident took place during a religious ritual, and no group claimed responsibility[51].

A Shia scholar, Allama Ali Akbar Kumaili, and his bodyguard were shot dead[52].

September 9: Sabir Hussain and his son Ghulam Hussain were shot dead by terrorists of Sipah-e Sahaba in Orangi Town Area of Karachi[53].

September 10: Mohammad Zubair with his three-year-old son, Mohammad Dauf was shot dead near Ghareeb Shah Shrine in Kalakot, Lyari[54].

September 11: A religious teacher, Dr Maulana Masood Baig, was shot dead in North Nazimabad, and two activist of the Muttahida Qaumi Movement were gunned down in Khuda Ki Basti.

In the second such killing, Imran Ali, 35, was gunned down in a Surjani Town locality.

In the third attack, another Shia man Salman Kazmi, was gunned down in a firing incident in District Central of Karachi[55].

September 15: A Shia cleric, Syed Mohsin Raza Jaffri, 70, was shot dead outside his residence in Latifabad town[56].

September 19: Mohammad Shakil Auj, a 54-year-old professor of Islam known for his liberal religious views has been killed in Karachi, two years after he was labelled an "apostate" in a text-message campaign[57].

September 27:   55-year-old bank employee Syed Ali Raza Zaidi was shot dead at his house in Hayatabad.

Deedar Ali Mughal s/o Basheer Ali was shot dead by terrorists of ASWJ in Khairpur district of Sindh province[58].

September 28: An officer of the special investigations unit, SSP, Farooq Awan was targeted in a car bomb attack in Karachi. Awan survived with minor injuries but two passers-by were killed and five other people were injured[59].

October 3: Three people were killed, and nine others injured when a roadside bomb hit a passenger van in Gilgit town[60].

October 4: A suicide attacker blew himself up in a Shia neighborhood of Quetta, killed three and injured 17[61].

October 6: Six Shias, Taimur, Syed Shah Zain, Eman, Shabbir Ali, Mehtab Hussain and Qamar Abbas were killed and 17 others injured in Kohat.

Shia journalist Nadeem Haider was killed in Hafizabad area of Punjab province.

48 "Another Shia Muslim shot martyred in Karachi," *ShiaPost*. August 29, 2014, http://en.shiapost.com/2014/08/29/another-shia-muslim-shot-martyred-in-karachi/.
49 "Pakistan: 28 doctors mostly Shiite killed in targeted attacks over four years," *Shia Waves*. August 30, 2014, http://shiawaves.com/english/islam/251-28-pakistani-doctors-mostly-shias-killed-in-targeted-attacks-over-four-years.
50 "2 More Shia Muslims Killed in Karachi – Pakistan," *AhlulBayt News Agency*. September 7, 2014, http://www.abna.ir/english/service/centeral-asia-subcontinent/archive/2014/09/07/636061/story.html.
51 "Shia army officer and 2 others shot dead by gunmen in Pakistan," *FirstPost*. September 8, 2014, http://www.firstpost.com/world/shia-army-officer-2-others-shot-dead-by-gunmen-in-pakistan-1701929.html.
52 "Pakistanis protest against Shia killings," *PressTV*. September 8, 2014, http://www.presstv.ir/detail/2014/09/08/378033/pakistanis-protest-against-shia-killings/.
53 "Pakistan: Terrorists killed a Shia man and his son in Karachi," *Jafri News*. September 9, 2014, http://jafrianews.com/tag/karachi/.
54 "Father, toddler among seven shot dead," *TheNews*. September 10, 2014, http://www.thenews.com.pk/Todays-News-4-271924-Father-toddler-among-seven-shot-dead.
55 "Pakistan: A Sunni Cleric, and two Shiite activists shot dead, Police arrest killer of 40 Shiite Muslims," *AhlulBayt News Agency*. September 11, 2014, http://www.abna.ir/english/service/centeral-asia-subcontinent/archive/2014/09/11/637050/story.html.
56 "Head of local Shia organisation shot dead in Hyderabad, Pakistan," *Daily Times*. September 15, 2014, http://www.dailytimes.com.pk/national/15-Sep-2014/shia-leader-shot-dead-in-hyderabad.
57 "Liberal academic killed in Pakistan's Karachi,"*Al Jazeera*. September 19, 2014, http://www.aljazeera.com/news/asia/2014/09/liberal-academic-killed-pakistan-karachi-201491962248583777.html.
58 "Two Shias Shot Killed in Pakistan," *AhlulBayt News Agency*. September 27, 2014, http://www.abna.ir/english/service/centeral-asia-subcontinent/archive/2014/09/27/640511/story.html.
59 "The attack on Karachi police; Shia and Sunni," *AhlulBayt News Agency*. September 28, 2014, http://www.abna.ir/english/service/centeral-asia-subcontinent/archive/2014/09/28/640787/story.html.
60 "Sectarian attack kills three Shias," *The Peninsula*. October 3, 2014, http://thepeninsulaqatar.com/news/pakistanafghanistan/302407/sectarian-attack-kills-three-shias.
61 "Police suicide attacker strikes Shia neighborhood in SW Pakistan killing 3," *Fox News*. October 4, 2014, http://www.foxnews.com/world/2014/10/04/police-suicide-attacker-strikes-shiite-neighborhood-in-sw-pakistan-killing-3/.

A Shia Hazara, Rehmatullah Atta Ali, 35, was shot by the Ahl-e-Sunnat-Wal-Jamaat (ASWJ) terrorists in Karachi's Manghopir area.

Zulfiqar Ali was shot by ASWJ terrorists in Orangi[62].

October 12: A Shia Muslim, Akbar Ali, was killed and another Shia Muslim Israf Ali was injured in a blast in the Sipah area of Orakzai.

October 16: A Shia Muslim was tortured to death in Faisalabad prison.

Terrorists of Sipah-e-Sahaba shot a Shia Muslim, Allah Ditta and injured his son Moin in Punjab province's Rahim Yar Khan District.

Another Shia Muslim, Muneer Raza was killed in Karachi.

October 20: Syed Ali Abbas Abedi, a Shia newspaper hawker, was shot dead in Joharabad, Karachi by SeS terrorists.

October 23: A bomb explosion in the city of Quetta killed three people and injured over a dozen[63].

Eight people died when a passenger bus carrying members of Shia minority Hazara community in the city of Quetta was attacked[64].

October 29: 9-month old Shia baby, Batool Waqar, was killed when Deobandi terrorists threw a hand grenade at a group of Shia women outside the Islamic Research Center mosque.

October 30: The police warned of possible terrorist attacks on different religious and political personalities in the country on occasion of 9 and 10 of Muharram.

November 2: A Shia activist of Payam-e-Wilayat-Foundation Wajid Hussain, 22, was targeted in his car near Mumtaz Manzil, Hassan Square area of Karachi.

Hussain's friend Ali Imran is critically injured.

Allah Dino Mallah and Sunil Sothar were sprayed bullets and killed.

Three others including Mir Noman Talpur and Mahboob Mari sustained critical wounds.

November 6: Tufail Haider, a Shia Muslim, was killed by a Pakistani policeman in a frenzied ax attack over allegedly blasphemous comments about companions of Prophet Mohammed[65].

November 7: Sahar Batool, a six-year-old Hazara girl was murdered after rape attempts[66].

November 8: A 35-year-old Shia Cleric, Nasir Abbas was killed in Gulbahar area of Peshawar by terrorists of ASWJ[67].

November 13: Maulana Shafqat Abbas Mutaheri, a Shia leader, was shot dead in Khanpur town of Shikarpur district.

At least five people, two of them Shias, were killed while two others were critically wounded when unknown armed assailants opened fire at multiple shops on Usman Road in Balochi Street of Quetta.

3 Shia Muslims including a senior Shia citizen Syed Johar shah, aged 70-years, were shot dead in Charsadha[68].

November 18: A Shia student and a driver were killed and five other students wounded in a roadside explosion near a school van in Nasti Kot area of Kurram tribal region's Parachinar district[69].

[62] "Saudi-Backed Terrorists Butchered 14 Shia Muslims on Eid al Adha in Pakistan," *AhlulBayt News Agency*. October 6, 2014, http://www.abna.ir/english/service/centeral-asia-subcontinent/archive/2014/10/06/642491/story.html.
[63] "Bomb attack kills 3 in Pakistan," *PressTV*. October 23, 2014, http://www.presstv.ir/detail/2014/10/23/383351/bomb-attack-kills-3-in-pakistan.
[64] "Gunmen attack minority Shia Muslims in Pakistan," *Wall Street Journal*. October 23, 2014, http://online.wsj.com/articles/gunmen-attack-minority-shia-muslims-in-pakistan-1414051262.
[65] "Pakistani cop hacks detainee to death with ax for 'blasphemy'," *RT*. November 6, 2014, http://rt.com/news/202859-pakistan-blasphemy-policeman-kills/.
[66] "Six-year-old Hazara girl murdered in Quetta after attempted rape," *Dawn*. November 7, 2014, http://www.dawn.com/news/1142905/six-year-old-hazara-girl-murdered-in-quetta-after-attempted-rape.
[67] "Pakistani Shia Cleric Allama Nasir Abbas martyred by ASWJ terrorists on Peshawar," *ByIslam*. November 8, 2014, http://www.byislam.com/site/?p=5730.
[68] "Six Shias shot martyred in Pakistan," *AhlulBayt News Agency*. November 13, 2014, http://www.abna.ir/english/service/centeral-asia-subcontinent/archive/2014/11/13/651106/story.html.
[69] "Pakistan: Shia student, driver martyred in roadside blast in Parachinar," *The Shia Post* November 18, 2014, http://en.shiapost.com/2014/11/18/shia-student-driver-martyred-in-roadside-blast-in-parachinar/.

November 19: A Shia custodian on Jahanian shrine was killed by ASWJ terrorists in an area between Multan and Khanewal districts of Punjab province[70].

November 20: Syed Arshad Ali Shah, a Shia police officer, was shot dead in Wadpaga village of Khyber-Pukhtoonkhwa province[71].

November 22: Muhammad Aslam Lehri, a newly converted Shia Muslim was targeted outside his home in Azizabad area in Mastung, Balochistan.

November 27: Shabbir Hussain, a shop keeper in Quetta, was shot killed by ASWJ terrorists.

Two Shia Muslims were killed in Sindh and one was killed in Balochistan.

November 28: A Shia cleric, Allama Nawaz Irfani, was shot dead in Islamabad[72].

November 29: The sectarian terrorist organization, Jundullah, claimed responsibility for the attack that killed four polio workers in Quetta[73].

December 2: 58-year old Shia doctor, Shamim Raza, was shot dead in his clinic in Korangi, Karachi.

Two Shia police cops Ali Hassan, 38, and Mir Hassan, 35, were injured when ASWJ terrorists opened fire upon them in central Karachi.

December 3: A Shia Muslim of Parachinar, Jabir Hussain, was kidnapped, tortured during the captivity and assassinated by ASWJ terrorists.

ASWJ terrorists attacked and injured another Shia Muslim, Dr. Baqar Raza, in North Nazimabad district of Karachi[74].

December 6: Gunmen killed a trader from Shia community and injured a passerby at the busy commercial area of Parda Bagh near Bacha Khan Chowk[75].

December 11: Shia Muslim of Parachinar, who sustained critical wounds in a blast in June 2013, died after more than 17 months of treatment.

December 16: Seven members of the TTP conducted a terrorist attack on the Army Public School in the city of Peshawar by opening fire on school staff and children and killing 145 people regardless of ethnicity or religion.

December 17: A Shia scholar, Allama Sadiq Raza Taqvi, escaped unhurt from the attack of ASWJ terrorists in Gulistan-e-Johar. His guard was injured[76].

December 20: Two Shia brothers, Syed Adnan Raza Rizvi and Imran Raza Rizvi, were killed in Karachi.

Another Shia was killed in Mastung, Balochistan by ASWJ terrorists.

December 24: A Shia trader and his friend, Aun Naqvi and Mathir Jafferi, were killed and Saleem Hussain was injured in the Gulberg area of Karachi.

December 29: Muslim Mahdavi, a Shia noha reciter, was injured by ASWJ terrorirsts in Karimabad, Karachi.

[70] "Pakistan: A Shia custodian on Jahanian shrine martyred by takfiri terrorists," *Shiite News*. November 19, 2014, http://www.shiitenews.org/index.php/shiitenews/pakistan/shia-custodian-of-jahanian-shrine-martyred-by-takfiri-terrorists.
[71] "A Shia police constable martyred in Peshawar," *AhlulBayt News Agency*. November 20, 2014, http://www.abna.ir/english/service/centeral-asia-subcontinent/archive/2014/11/20/652522/story.html.
[72] "Pakistani Shia cleric shot dead in Islamabad," *Channel News Asia*. November 28, 2014, http://www.channelnewsasia.com/news/asiapacific/pakistani-shia-cleric/1499696.html.
[73] "Jundullah claims attack, again," *Nation*. November 29, 2014, http://nation.com.pk/editorials/29-Nov-2014/jundullah-claims-attack-again.
[74] "Takfiri terrorists killed a Shia, injured a doctor in two separate attacks in Pakistan," *Islamic News World Wide*. December 3, 2014, http://islamicnewsworldwide.blogspot.com/2014/12/shia-noha-reciter-injured-in-takfiri.html
[75] "Gunmen shot dead Shia trader in Peshawar-Pakistan," *AhlulBayt News Agency*. December 6, 2014, http://www.abna.ir/english/service/centeral-asia-subcontinent/archive/2014/12/06/656203/story.html.
[76] "Pakistan: Shia scholar escapes unhurt, guard injured in takfiri terrorist attack," *AhlulBayt News Agency*. December 17, 2014, http://www.abna.ir/english/service/centeral-asia-subcontinent/archive/2014/12/17/658900/story.html.

According to Article 5 of International Bill of Human Rights (IBHR), "No one shall be subjected to torture or to cruel, inhuman or degrading treatment or punishment," but Shia are still at risk during their everyday lives.

January 7: Suspected Taliban militants tortured and killed six people in Karachi for visiting a Sufi shrine. Three of the victims were custodians for the shrine, whereas the other three came from varying parts of the city to visit. The Taliban believes that shrine and grave visiting is un-Islamic and therefore has sought to attack any who do. It was reported that the victims were kidnapped and tortured with a sharp-edged dagger before being killed and left at the scene, but not before they desecrated the shrine. They left a note for whoever found them saying that those who visited the shrines would suffer the same fate[77].

February 12: 76 Shia were taken into custody by so-called law enforcement agencies and are being held and tortured in the detention center[78].

March 18: Shia activist, Yawar Abbas Zaidi, and his two Sunni comrades were kidnapped at gunpoint twenty days previous and their tortured, bullet marked bodies were found in Nooriabad area [79].

April 24: Shia Murtaza Ali Bangash and his two Sunni friends were kidnapped and tortured, their bodies found in Karachi[80].

May 26: Punjab police arrested Khuwaja Mohammad Ali, a Shia leader, his wife, his two sister-in-laws, two children, his father, and a disabled Shia notable. Rawalpindi police tortured them, and they were taken to the Rawalpindi jail[81].

December 30: Syed Sikandar Rizvi, a Shia worker of a political party was kidnapped and tortured to death in Karachi[82].

VIOLATIONS OF THE RIGHT TO FREEDOM

The UDHR states in Article 9 that "No one shall be subjected to arbitrary arrest, detention or exile."

Pakistani President Mamnoon Hussain on July 11 gave Pakistani citizens a new reason to fear the country's security forces. He signed into law the Protection of Pakistan Act, whose provisions open the door for the violation of fundamental rights to freedom of speech, privacy, peaceful assembly and a fair trial.

Although the law has just a two-year mandate, it could quickly be used to suppress peaceful political opposition and criticism of government policy. The non-governmental Human Rights Commission of Pakistan rightly described the law as a 'blatant attack on the fundamental rights of the people'. The law violates fundamental rights enshrined in the International Covenant on Civil and Political Rights (ICCPR), which Pakistan ratified in 2010[83].

VICTIMS OF ARBITRARY DETENTION

January 25: SP CID Police officially announce the illegal holding of two Shia, Johar Hussain, who had been held since 6 December 2013, and Irshad. Johar's wife, Shabia Sultana, filed a report on her missing husband after getting a call to arrange Rs. 200,000 for his release, to which she replied that the money would get to them, but only after she saw her detained husband. When she and her husband's friend, Irshad, visited Johar, they detained Irshad as well, saying that the Rs. 200,000 would release both of them, but if it were delayed, they would both be implicated[84].

February 12: 76 Shia are being held in Rawalpindi jail and reported as tortured[85].

[77] "Six slaughtered in Karachi over Sufi shrine visit," *UCA News*. January 7, 2014, http://www.ucanews.com/news/six-slaughtered-in-karachi-over-sufi-shrine-visit/70032.
[78] "MWM to launch movement against pro-Taliban govt. policies," *Shia Post*. January 16, 2014, http://en.shiapost.com/2014/02/16/mwm-to-launch-movement-against-pro-taliban-govt-policies/.
[79] "Pakistan: Infidel of Sipah-e-Sahaba shot killed 2 Shia Muslims," *AhlulBayt News Agency*. March 19, 2014, http://www.abna.ir/english/service/important/archive/2014/03/19/514390/story.html.
[80] "Shia sympathizer of a political party martyred along with Sunni friends," *Shiite News*. April 24, 2014, http://www.shiitenews.com/index.php/pakistan/9762-shia-sympathizer-of-a-political-party-martyred-along-with-sunni-friends.
[81] "Punjab police detains 8 Shias including 3 women, 2 minors and a disabled," *Shia Post*. May 25, 2014, http://en.shiapost.com/2014/05/26/punjab-police-detains-8-shias-including-3-women-2-minors-a-disable/.
[82] "Shia worker of a political party kidnapped and martyred in Karachi," *Ahlul Bayt News Agency*. December 30, 2014, http://www.abna.ir/english/service/central-asia-subcontinent/archive/2014/12/30/661662/story.html.
[83] Phelim Kine. "Pakistan's Dangerous Anti-Terrorism Law." *Human Rights Watch*. (June 2014).
[84] "SP CID claims to arrest 2 innocent Shia youths who were already under his illegal detention for 50 days," *Shiite News*. January 25, 2014, http://www.shiitenews.com/index.php/pakistan/8831-sp-cid-claims-to-arrest-2-innocent-shia-youths-who-were-already-under-his-illegal-detention-for-50-days.
[85] *Shia Post*. January 16, 2014.

March 13: SeS/ASWJ terrorists attacked Saeed ul Hassan Rizvi, a local Shia leader, to divert attention from their blasphemous graffiti and accused him for contempt of companions of Prophet, a baseless charge militants usually put on Muslims[86].

March 15: Top leaders of Majlis-e-Wahdat-e-Muslmeen and 60 others were detained the day before their scheduled anti-Taliban conference, Labbaik Ya Rasoolullah[87].

March 18: Police arrested Syed Mohammad Raza Shah in his bookstore for selling Nehjul Balaghah, a book of sermons and sayings of Imam Ali who is considered by the Shia Muslims to be the first leader after Prophet Muhammad. Lahore police had already filed a complaint and wanted the bookstore owner to be arrested for banning SeS's fanatics in his shop[88].

March 24: Allama Asif Raza Alvi was arrested for speaking the truth on the tyrannies and despotism of dynastic rulers of Umayyad who seized power, bringing an end to the Caliphate[89].

April 12: Shia scholar, Allama Waheed Abbas Kazmi, and high official, Nayyar Abbas Jafari, were arrested under Maintenance of Public Order (MPO) for exercising their inalienable rights that are guaranteed to everyone under Pakistan's Constitution[90].

May 13: 68 lawyers are being charged after a protest against Officer Umar Daraz who illegally detained and beat one of their colleagues. The charge states that they were using derogatory language towards Caliph Umar himself, not Officer Umar[91].

May 26: Eight arrested by Punjabi police, including a notable Shia leader[92].

November 16: Police of district Shikarpur has registered a false case against the 300 Shia Muslims for their peaceful sit-in to protest against the brutal assassination of Allama Shafqat Abbas Mutahri.

ON ARBITRARY INTERFERENCE WITH PRIVACY

Article 12 of the Human Rights Declarations states "No one shall be subjected to arbitrary interference with his privacy, family, home or correspondence, or to attacks upon his honor and reputation. Everyone has the right to the protection of the law against such interference or attacks."

January 30: Vice Principal Syed Asghan Hussain Zaidi killed and wife injured after ASWJ attack[93].

April 16: Militant group dropped pamphlets in Peshawar village, consisting mostly of Shia, to vacate the area within ten days or they would fall victim94. Three days later, the village was attacked; Shia and Sunnis fought together against the terrorists for twenty minutes before the militants fled[95].

May 26: Eight arrested by Punjabi police, including notable Shia leader[96].

ON FREEDOM OF RELIGION

Previously mentioned violations also fell under Article 18: "Everyone has the right to freedom of thought, conscience and religion; this right includes freedom to change his religion or belief, and freedom, either alone or in community with others and in public or private, to manifest his religion or belief in teaching, practice, worship and observance."

[86] "Yazidi terrorists attack Shia leader in a bid to hide their blasphemous graffiti," Shia Post. March 13, 2014, http://en.shiapost.com/2014/03/14/yazidi-terrorists-attack-shia-leader-in-a-bid-to-hide-their-blasphemous-graffiti/.
[87] "MWMs top leaders 60 others arrested in Khairpur," Shia Post. March 15, 2014, http://en.shiapost.com/2014/03/15/mwms-top-leaders-60-others-arrested-in-khairpur/.
[88] "Pakistan: Shia publisher arrested for selling Nehjul Balaghah," AhlulBayt News Agency. March 18, 2014, http://www.abna.co/data.asp?lang=3&Id=514337.
[89] "Shia scholar held for narrating truth about tyrannies of Umayyad despotic rule," Shiite News. March 24, 2014, http://www.shiitenews.com/index.php/pakistan/9355-shia-scholar-held-for-narrating-truth-about-tyrannies-of-umayyad-despotic-rule.
[90] "Shia scholar and officer detained under MPO by biased Haripur admin," Shiite News. April 12, 2014, http://www.shiitenews.com/index.php/pakistan/9618-shia-scholar-and-officer-detained-under-mpo-by-biased-haripur-admin.
[91] "Pakistan lawyers charged en masse with blasphemy," UCA News. May 13, 2014, http://www.ucanews.com/news/pakistan-lawyers-charged-en-masse-with-blasphemy/70922.
[92] Shia Post. May 25, 2014.
[93] Shia Post. January 31, 2014.
[94] "Shia Muslim neighborhood threatened in Pakistan," UCA News. April 16, 2014, http://www.ucanews.com/news/shia-muslim-neighborhood-threatened-in-pakistan/70725.
[95] "Takfiri terrorists attack on Shias near Peshawar, more attacks planned," Shia Post. April 16, 2014, http://en.shiapost.com/2014/04/19/takfiri-terrorists-attack-on-shiites-near-peshawar-more-attacks-planned/.
[96] Shia Post. May 25, 2014.

Despite the fact that the Council of Islamic Ideology (CII) in Pakistan today appeals to Muslims to stop spreading hatred such as branding other sects as 'non-believers', in an effort to prevent violence against the Shia population, Shias of Pakistan are still oppressed by the extremists[97].

January 7: Six people killed by Taliban militants for visiting Sufi shrine in Karachi[98].

March 18: Bookstore owner arrested for selling a book of sermons and sayings of Imam Ali.

March 14: The Shia conference, Labbaik Ya Rasoolullah, leaders were arrested before the conference took place, hoping to dishearten those that planned to attend, and in an effort to advertise the conference, seven Shia youth were injured by SeS/ASWJ militants who opened fire[99].

June 6: The Pakistan government banned the Shiite News website and Facebook page[100].

September 22: ASWJ set a Shia mosque on fire on Sunday in Rawalpindi[101].

October 14: Liaquat Ali Hazara, a campaigner for Shia rights, despite being in the UK, receives death threats from Taliban[102].

October 28: Pakistani Shia leader, Syed Ghulam Raza Naqvi, is released after being imprisoned for 18 years without any charges.

December 4: The Crisis Management Cell alerted the relevant officials of the government that Ahmed Farooq group of al-Qaeda was active and planned to assassinate Shia religious scholars, Shia politicians, Shia traders, and Shia professionals and Shia notables. Alongside, the takfiri terrorists of al-Qaeda also planned to hit Shia mosques and Imam Bargahs[103].

CONCLUSION

The Shia community in Pakistan has always been discriminated against for their religion and the government has done nothing to protect them as they are attacked on a daily basis. As a member of the United Nations, Pakistan has agreed to and accepted the Universal Declaration of Human Rights, but it is clear that these rights are being violated continuously. Terrorist groups such as the LeJ, SeS, ASWJ, and the Pakistani Taliban believe that Shia Muslims have been given too much importance, and being given senior positions- scholars, doctors, lawyers, politicians. For that reason, they mostly target Shia scholars, activists or those who have senior positions.

In 2014, at least 210 members of the Shia Muslim population were killed in targeted attacks that took place across Pakistan; around half of the amount from the neighboring provinces of Balochistan and Sindh. The deaths that are not targeted killings carried by the sectarian terrorist groups (LeJ, SeS, TTP) are cases of torture by the police.

Besides the violations of right to life, Pakistani Shias suffer violations of right to freedom as well. They are often subjected to arbitrary detention and arbitrary interference of privacy. The recently signed Protection of Pakistan Act opens the door to carry the violations of fundamental rights to freedom of speech, privacy, peaceful assembly and fair trial in a more systematic and official way. Moreover, there is no freedom of religion for Shia Muslims. Visiting a shrine, attending a conference, reading a book about Shiism or any gathering of the Shia Muslims can become a reason of death or imprisonment.

The ideology that considers Shias as infidels has attracted media attention by the recent brutal actions of the ISIS. The same ideology exists in Pakistan. Although there is no significant connection between ISIS and the local Pakistani sectarian terrorist groups at this time, the situation in Pakistan has potential to become worse if any alliance is formed between the two groups that

[97] "Pak Islamic body seeks curb on hate speech to check violence," *Business Standard*. October 22, 2014, http://www.business-standard.com/article/pti-stories/pak-islamic-body-seeks-curbs-on-hate-speech-to-check-violence-114102200775_1.html.
[98] *UCA News*. January 7, 2014.
[99] "7 Shia youths injured in Yazidi terrorists attack in Khairpur," *Shiite News*. March 14, 2014, http://www.shiitenews.com/index.php/pakistan/9263-7-shia-youths-injured-in-yazidi-terrorist-attack-in-khairpur.
[100] "Government banned Shiite news Facebook page after website," *Shiite News*. June 6, 2014, http://www.shiitenews.com/index.php/pakistan/10248-govt-banned-shiite-news-facebook-page-after-website.
[101] "ASWJ set Shia mosque on fire," *AhlulBayt News Agency*. September 22, 2014, http://www.abna.ir/english/service/central-asia-subcontinent/archive/2014/09/22/639295/story.html.
[102] "UK deport Pakistani activist Liaquat Ali Hazara," *The Guardian*. October 14, 2014, http://www.theguardian.com/world/2014/oct/14/uk-deport-pakistani-activist-liaquat-ali-hazara.
[103] "Pakistan: Shia mosques and Imam Bargahs under threat from takfiri terrorists," *AhlulBayt News Agency*. December 4, 2014, http://www.abna.ir/english/service/central-asia-subcontinent/archive/2014/12/04/655828/story.html.

share the same ideology and hatred against the Shia Muslims. On November 18, a spokesperson for Jundullah, a splinter group of Pakistan's Taliban, confirmed the group's support to Islamic State by saying "they (Islamic State) are our brothers, whatever plan they have we will support them". If such an alliance is formed, brutality of the ISIS spreads into the Asian subcontinent, and the Shia population of Pakistan faces harsher consequences.

Therefore, in order to end the brutal actions of LeJ and SeS and prevent any alliance between these terrorist groups and ISIS, the Pakistani government should be in collaboration with the international actors as well as the non-governmental organizations.

KEY RECOMMENDATIONS

The Pakistan government should take immediate measures to investigate and prosecute sectarian killings and conduct a broader investigation into sectarian killings. Specifically, Shia Rights Watch urges:

To the Government of Pakistan

• Prime Minister should follow up on his public denunciations of sectarian killings by ordering the immediate arrest and prosecution of the leadership of the LeJ, its members, and affiliates responsible for planning, ordering, perpetrating, inciting, or enabling sectarian violence.

• Disband, disarm, and hold accountable all militant groups implicated in serious human rights violations, particularly the LeJ.

• Establish an independent federal commission to investigate, recommend criminal prosecutions, and publicly report on sectarian killings in the Shia dominated provinces. The commission should investigate the failure of successive Pakistani governments at the federal, provincial, and local levels to successfully investigate and prosecute such sectarian killings in Shia neighborhoods. The commission should be given authority to hold public hearings and subpoena individuals, including survivors of sectarian attacks, relatives of victims, government officials, and security force personnel, to testify.

Immediately remove from service any administrative or security personnel implicated in sectarian attacks or who failed to investigate and arrest alleged perpetrators of such attacks.

Take extra security measures in Balochistan and Sindh provinces as the majority of the terrorist attacks against Shias take place in these provinces.

Take security measures in borders in order to prevent any activity between the local terrorist groups and globally known terrorists groups that share the same ideology.

TO INTERNATIONAL ACTORS

• Press the Pakistani government to uphold its international human rights obligations and promote good governance by investigating sectarian killings in Shia dominant areas and prosecuting all those responsible, particularly the LeJ leadership, which has publicly claimed responsibility for hundreds of attacks.

• Press the Pakistani government to disband, disarm, and hold accountable all militant groups implicated in serious human rights violations.

• Offer to support external law enforcement assistance with investigations into sectarian killings in Shia dominant areas.

• Use bilateral meetings, including within the diplomatic, law enforcement, and intelligence realms, to reinforce these messages.

• Communicate to the Pakistani authorities that a failure to take action against militant groups implicated in abuses against minorities in areas under government control jeopardizes international economic, development, and military assistance and cooperation.

To Non-Governmental Organizations

Restore/ preserve all destroyed Shia mosques and shrines

Initiate human rights training

Initiate religious tolerance at a young age

Promote dialogue between the Sunnis and Shias.

GLOSSARY

Ahle Sunnat Wal Jamaat(ASWJ): An anti-Shia terrorist group that is being referred to when LeJ and SeS are banded together.

Frontier Corps: The Frontier Corps is a federal auxiliary paramilitary force that acts as a unit of the Pakistan Army. It is led by senior serving army officers but falls under the formal jurisdiction of Pakistan's federal interior ministry.

Islamic State of Iraq and Syria (ISIS): ISIS is a Sunni, extremist, jihadist, unrecognized state and self-proclaimed caliphate based in Iraq and Syria.

Lashkar-e-Jhangvi (LeJ): The LEJ is a militant extremist Sunni Deobandi group formed in 1996 as a breakaway faction of the sectarian militant Sipah-e-Sahaba Pakistan (SSP). The LeJ views Shia Muslims as heretics and their killing as religiously justified.

Maintenance of Public Order (MPO): The MPO ordinance is a preventive detention measure that allows the state to override standard legal procedures and due process of law in situations in which the government deems any person a threat to public order or safety. It allows the government to "arrest and detain suspected persons" for up to six months for a range of offenses.

Majlis-e-Wahdat-e-Muslimeen: Biggest religious-political Shia Party in Pakistan.

Muharram: Muharram is the first month of the Islamic calendar, which the Shia community marks with a variety of mass outdoor religious rituals mourning the massacre of Prophet Mohammad's grandson and his family. The event marks the origin of the Shia-Sunni schism in Islam.

Sipah-e-Sahaba Pakistan (SSP): The SSP is a militant Sunni Deobandi group formed in 1980 with the declared aim of containing Shia influence in Pakistan after the 1979 Iranian revolution.

Sunni Deobandi school of thought: The Deobandi school of thought in Islam came to prominence with the founding in 1866 in India of Darul Uloom Deoband, regarded as the first "modern" Islamic Madrassah. It advocates a hardline Sunni interpretation of Islam as practiced by the Taliban.

Tehrik-e Taliban Pakistan (TPP): The TTP is a militant Islamist umbrella group claiming inspiration from the Afghan Taliban, though it is operationally autonomous. It formally declared its existence in 2007. It and affiliated groups are responsible for the deaths of tens of thousands of Pakistani civilians and more than 10,000 military personnel.